HOW TO PLAY WORLD-BEAT RHYTHMS WITH JUST YOUR BODY AND A BUDDY

by Alan Dworsky and Betsy Sansby

Cover art by Toni Pawlowsky

DANCING HANDS MUSIC

Slap Happy: How to Play World-Beat Rhythms with Just Your Body and a Buddy

Published by
DANCING HANDS MUSIC
4275 Churchill Circle
Minnetonka, MN 55345
phone or fax: 952-933-0781
dancinghands.com

Cover art by Toni Pawlowsky

Illustrations by Toni Pawlowsky (pages 1, 16, 19, 26 and 33), Jay Kendell (pages 24, 28, 40, 43, 48 and 56), and Robert Jackson (pages 13, 30, 31, 54 and 55)

Book design and layout by Mighty Media

Printed in the United States of America
with soy ink on recycled, acid-free paper by Banta ISG (Viking Press)

Slapping patterns on the CD performed by Betsy Sansby and Alan Dworsky

Drum tracks on the CD performed by Marc Anderson and Alan Dworsky

ISBN 0-9638801-7-9

THIS BOOK IS DEDICATED TO MARK MODAFFERI,
every kid's dream of a music teacher,
and to his lucky students at
Cato-Meridian Central School in Cato, New York.

Table of Contents

What is Slap Happy?

SLAP HAPPY is a fun way to turn drum rhythms into body rhythms you can step, clap, and slap with a buddy. Right from the start, you'll be learning how to slap traditional rhythms from West Africa and the Caribbean: Kuku from Guinea, Sunguru Bani from Mali, Kpegisu from Ghana, Bomba from Puerto Rico, and Conga from Cuba.

You can do Slap Happy in pairs or in groups, indoors or out, at home or at school. If you're a parent, it's a great way to do something fun and educational with your kids that doesn't require any previous musical training.

If you're a music teacher, you can use Slap Happy to give your students a hands-on experience of world rhythms without having to buy any instruments. And while the kids are learning the rhythms, they'll be building co-ordination, concentration, and cooperation.

Here's how it works. The book is organized into lessons that are arranged in order of difficulty. Each lesson includes several patterns related to a single rhythm. The patterns start simple and gradually get more complex. But you'll hardly notice, because we make sure you get the right-size steps, in the right order, at just the right time.

The first step with each new pattern is to learn to slap it solo. The next step is to learn to slap it with a buddy. The final step is to combine patterns to create the Slap Happy version of an African or Afro-Caribbean drum ensemble.

The charts we use are easy to understand even if you've never read music before. And we don't just dump a pile of charts on you and leave. We'll be with you every step of the way, anticipating your questions, pointing out whatever is most important, and explaining whatever we think will make your journey easier.

The CD that comes with the book has a recording of every rhythm you'll be learning, so you can hear how each pattern is supposed to sound. You can also slap along with the special extended recordings of each rhythm played on congas, djembes, and other traditional drums. For easy reference, you'll find the numbers of all the slap-along drum tracks on the face of the CD itself.

Slap Happy was designed to embody the spirit of world rhythms and make people laugh. We hope it does both for you.

The charts and the moves

We use box charts for Slap Happy because they're simple, clear, and easy to read. We could have used standard music notation, the kind you're familiar with if you play an instrument or sing in a chorus. But standard music notation gives you lots of information you don't need for Slap Happy, like the pitch of a note and how long to hold it. All you need to know to start slapping is *what* move to make and *when* to make it.

That's what our three-row box charts tell you. Let's take a look at one:

KUKU PART 1 (SOLO)   **TRACKS 4 & 5**

1	+	2	+	3	+	4	+	1	+	2	+	3	+	4	+
ᵀ				ᵀ				H		H		H	H		
👣				👣				👣				👣			

Above the chart you'll see the name of the pattern and the word "solo" or "buddy" in parentheses. You'll also see track numbers that tell you where you can hear the pattern on the CD.

If there's only one track number, that means you'll hear the pattern slapped on that track. If there are two track numbers – as on the chart above – you'll hear the pattern slapped on the first track and drummed on the second. The slap tracks are just long enough to give you an idea of how a pattern is supposed to sound. The drum tracks are a full two minutes long, to give you plenty of time to slap along.

The top row of the chart – the count row – tells you how to count a rhythm. Time moves from left to right, with each box being a single beat. The symbol "+" stands for "AND," so to count this rhythm you'd say "1 AND 2 AND 3 AND 4 AND." Each chart is two measures long, so the count repeats twice on the count row at the top of each chart.

All the rhythms you'll be learning are dance rhythms that are meant to be repeated over and over. So think of every chart as if it were written in a circle. When you get to the end, go right back to the beginning and start over without missing a beat.

Think of every chart as if it were written in a circle. When you get to the end, go right back to the beginning and start over without missing a beat.

The shaded boxes on the count row tell you where the pulse is in a rhythm. The **pulse** is the steady rhythm people feel in their bodies when music is playing. When you tap your feet to a song, you're tapping the pulse. When you dance, your feet move to the pulse. In the chart above, you can see that the pulse falls on beats 1 and 3.

Since the pulse is so fundamental to rhythm, we're going to have you step it with every pattern in this book (except for the last lesson, when you'll be stepping a more complex pattern). Each step is indicated by a foot in a box on the bottom row of each chart – the foot row. As you can see, in the chart above you step the pulse on beats 1 and 3 – the same beats that are shaded on the count row. It doesn't matter which foot you start with as long as you alternate feet. And you won't be moving around; you'll just be stepping in place.

That just leaves the middle row – the hand row. It tells you what to do with your hands and when to do it. Each letter stands for a move. For example, "**T**" stands for "double thigh." So in this rhythm, on beats 1 and 3 in the first measure you'll slap both your thighs with both hands.

Here's a list of all the Slap Happy moves and the letters or symbols we use for them. Don't worry about memorizing them right now. We'll explain each one as we go along:

Π	=	double thigh
T	=	thigh
H	=	heart
C	=	clap
S	=	slap
X	=	snap
P	=	patty
F	=	flip
✳	=	splash
ϡ	=	step

That's all you need to know for now. So let's get cracking and start slapping!

Lesson # Kuku

The first rhythm you're going to learn comes from the West African country of Guinea. It's called Kuku (KOO-KOO) and it's a dance rhythm of celebration.

Kuku – like most African rhythms – is like an intricate puzzle, with interlocking parts that all fit together. In this lesson, you'll learn how to slap two of the parts that are traditionally played on djembes. A **djembe** (jem-bay) is a goblet-shaped drum carved from a single piece of wood with a drumhead made from goat skin. You can hear the two parts you're going to learn played on djembes on Track 1 on the CD.

Your first solo slapping pattern is a warm-up exercise. It's a simplified version of one of the drum parts you just heard. We've made this pattern as easy as possible to help you get used to coordinating your hands and feet. Before you try it, let's take a look at the chart and go over the moves:

1	+	2	+	3	+	4	+	1	+	2	+	3	+	4	+
⫪				⫪				H				H			
👣				👣				👣				👣			

⫪ = double thigh

The "⫪" stands for **double thigh**. All you do is slap both thighs at once. Be sure to slap just hard enough to get a good sound. Don't smack yourself so hard you hurt your legs.

H = heart

The "**H**" stands for **heart**. All you do is thump the center of your chest with your palm. Hearts are done one hand at a time, first right then left. Try to keep your hands loose and relaxed. The idea is to get a low thud – like the sound of a bass drum – not to knock the wind out of yourself.

👣 = step

The "👣" stands for **step**. All you do is step in place. You can step standing or sitting, but standing is more fun because it gives your body more freedom to move. (If standing is a problem, you can step all the patterns sitting down.)

SLAPPING PRINCIPLE

Go easy. Don't slap yourself so hard it hurts.

When you step, it doesn't matter which foot you start on as long as you alternate feet. If you're standing, make sure you bend your knees and lift your feet off the floor. It's hard to really feel the pulse if your legs are stiff and you're just rocking from side to side like Frankenstein.

SLAPPING
PRINCIPLE

If standing is a
problem, you can
step all the
patterns while
sitting down.

Bend your knees and lift your feet off the floor. Don't just rock from side to side like Frankenstein.

Lifting your feet off the floor will also help you to *hear* the pulse, especially when you're wearing shoes. If you have a choice, a wood floor is ideal for Slap Happy because it resonates. Carpet muffles your steps and concrete gets hard on your feet.

Before you try the first pattern, we just want to point out a couple more things. Here's the chart again:

KUKU PART 1 – WARM-UP 1 (SOLO)   **TRACK 2**

1	+	2	+	3	+	4	+	1	+	2	+	3	+	4	+
T				T				H				H			
👣				👣				👣				👣			

Notice that every move falls on a pulse, so you'll be stepping and slapping at the same time. The only thing that's a little tricky is that when you do the thighs, you'll slap with both hands at the same time but when you do the hearts, you'll slap with one hand and then the other. So the hand pattern goes: together, together, right, left.

Now it's time give the pattern a try. Even though this is a solo pattern, it's a good idea to face whoever you're slapping with so you'll be in sync. If you're in a group, get in a circle so you can all see each other.

SLAPPING
PRINCIPLE

Even when you do
solo patterns, face
whoever you're
slapping with so
you'll be in sync.

Start by counting out loud together while you get a slow, steady pulse going in your feet on 1 and 3. As you count, accent the pulse in your voice: "**1** AND 2 AND **3** AND 4 AND ..." Once you're stepping in sync, then add the hand moves. That's what you'll hear us doing on Track 2.

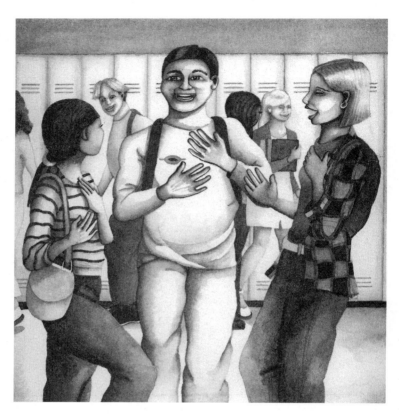

SLAPPING
PRINCIPLE

If your feet are
tripping you up,
do the pattern
with just your
hands.

How did it go? Hands and feet working together? If your
feet are tripping you up, leave them out for now and just
do the patterns with your hands. You can always add the
feet later.

The next pattern is another warm-up exercise that will
bring you one slap closer to the first part from Kuku. All
you do is add one more heart. That's what you'll hear us
doing on Track 3.

SLAPPING
PRINCIPLE

Practice a pattern
by vocalizing it.

You'll also hear us **vocalizing** the pattern. Vocalizing has
been used for centuries by drummers around the world
to learn and memorize new patterns. In India, for example, there's a highly developed system for vocalizing
rhythms using nonsense syllables. A student may be
required to vocalize for a year or more before being
allowed to touch a drum.

The most obvious way to vocalize a slapping pattern is to call out each move in time, just as we do on Track 3: **"thighs, thighs, heart**-heart-**heart,** ..." (Whenever we write out a vocalization, words that fall on a pulse are printed in bold.) And from now on, each time we slap a new pattern on the CD, you'll hear us start by vocalizing it.

Here's how the second warm-up exercise looks on a chart. When you slap it, remember to alternate hands on the hearts – right-left-right:

KUKU PART 1 – WARM-UP 2 (SOLO)   **TRACK 3**

1	+	2	+	3	+	4	+	1	+	2	+	3	+	4	+
𝕋				𝕋				H		H		H			
👣				👣				👣				👣			

Now you're ready for the first part from Kuku. All you do is add one more heart on the AND of 3 in the second measure. You can hear this part slapped and vocalized on Track 4. You'll notice we vocalize the pattern two different ways: first with the moves and second with a phrase we stole from Mark Modafferi's kindergarten class. Of course, you can always make up any phrase you want when you're vocalizing. The goal is to find one that's easy to say and that makes the rhythm easy to remember. Our motto is: If you can rap it, you can slap it:

If you can rap it, you can slap it.

1	+	2	+	3	+	4	+	1	+	2	+	3	+	4	+
𝕋				𝕋				H		H		H	H		
👣				👣				👣				👣			

You can hear this pattern played on a djembe for a full two minutes on Track 5. So whenever you're ready, go ahead and slap along. (From now on, we won't usually remind you to listen to the CD or to slap along with the drum tracks. We'll assume you're doing it on your own.)

Once you've got the coordination and timing of a solo part down, you should have no trouble doing the buddy version. That's because the buddy version always has the same rhythm as the solo version. All that's different is that you change one or more hand moves to make contact with your partner.

SLAPPING
PRINCIPLE

Take off your
rings so you don't
hurt your buddy's
hands.

F = flip

So now grab a buddy who's about your height and stand facing each other a couple feet apart. Take off any rings you're wearing so you don't hurt your buddy's hands. And unless your buddy has a severe head cold, don't eat raw onions before slapping.

To turn the solo version of the first part from Kuku into the buddy version, all you're going to do is change the thighs to flips. To do a **flip**, put your arms out in front of you with your right palm down and your left palm up. Then – keeping your wrists nice and relaxed – just slap both your buddy's palms at the same time. Flips always come in pairs, so to do the second flip just turn your hands over and slap your buddy's palms again. (If you're working with younger kids, you can substitute patty-cakes – the move we call "patties" – for flips.)

SLAPPING
PRINCIPLE

If you're working
with younger kids,
substitute patties
for flips.

Remember to go easy on your buddy. Try to make contact on the flips without flipping out. Don't ever slap so hard you hurt your buddy's hands.

SLAPPING
PRINCIPLE

Don't slap so hard
you hurt your
buddy's hands.

Before you do a buddy pattern, you and your buddy need to get in sync. So start by counting out loud together nice and slow: "1 AND 2 AND 3 AND 4 AND ..." At the same time, get a pulse going in your feet. When you're sure you're in sync, give each other a nod and start slapping:

KUKU PART 1 (BUDDY)   **TRACKS 4 & 5**

1	+	2	+	3	+	4	+	1	+	2	+	3	+	4	+
F				F				H		H		H	H		
👣				👣				👣				👣			

SLAPPING PRINCIPLE

To get in sync with your buddy, count out loud together while you get a pulse going in your feet.

SLAPPING PRINCIPLE

Whenever the only contact in a buddy part is on flips you can do the part in a circle.

Notice that the track numbers on this chart are the same as the track numbers on the solo version. We didn't record any buddy versions on the CD because they sound almost the same as the solo versions. And anyway, by the time you get to a buddy version, you should be ready to go right to slapping along with the drum track. That track will always be the second track number on the chart – in this case Track 5.

By the way, if you've got three or more slappers, you can do this buddy part in a circle. In fact, whenever the only contact in a buddy part is on flips you can do the part in a circle. Just have everyone face the center and open up their arms to do the flips with the people on both sides of them.

Now we're going to move on to the second part from Kuku. Again – as with all the patterns in this book – you'll do the solo version before the buddy version. And just as we did with the first part from Kuku, we'll start with a warm-up exercise to get you ready. Here's the chart:

KUKU PART 2 – WARM-UP (SOLO)   **TRACK 6**

1	+	2	+	3	+	4	+	1	+	2	+	3	+	4	+
⏀		H	H	H		C		⏀		H	H	H		<u>C</u>	
👣				👣				👣				👣			

C = clap

An underlined letter on a chart means you start slapping the pattern on that beat.

The "**C**" stands for **clap**. All you do is clap your hands. That's easy enough. But notice that in this pattern the "C" on 4 in the second measure is underlined. Anytime a letter on a chart is underlined, it means you start slapping there. So with this pattern, you'll still start stepping and counting on 1 in the first measure, but you'll start *slapping* on 4 in the second. That's what you'll hear us do on Track 6.

It may feel a little strange at first to start slapping on 4. That's because in Western music, most rhythms start on 1. But in African music, different parts of the same rhythm are often staggered, so they start at different times – just like when you sing a round. This gives a rhythm a circular feeling, as if it has no clear beginning or end.

The way we vocalize this pattern on Track 6 should make it easier for you to feel it starting on 4. We use the phrase "you **must** pay the **rent**," with "you" falling on 4. If you can rap that phrase in time, you should have no trouble slapping the pattern.

To turn this warm-up pattern into the second part from Kuku, all you do is drop the third heart in each measure. That means the last heart you slap comes *right before* your foot hits the floor on 3. On Track 7, we first vocalize this pattern by calling out the moves. Then we rap it using the phrase "get **down** tonight" (which we took from an old disco song) with "get" falling on 4. Notice that the first hand move is still the clap on 4 in the second measure:

KUKU PART 2 (SOLO)   **TRACKS 7 & 8**

1	+	2	+	3	+	4	+	1	+	2	+	3	+	4	+
♪		H	H			C		♪		H	H			C	
♫				♫				♫				♫			

Remember: whenever there are two track numbers above a chart, the second number is the slap-along drum track. So if you want to slap part 2 from Kuku along with a djembe, put on Track 8.

Now that you know how to slap both solo parts from Kuku, it's time for you and your buddy to put them together. One of you will slap part 1 while the other slaps part 2. Here's how it works.

First get in sync by counting and stepping together, just as if you were going to do a buddy part. Then have whoever's slapping part 1 start slapping first. After a repetition or two, whoever's slapping part 2 should come in on 4 in the second measure. That's what you'll hear on Track 9. Once you can slap the two solo parts together comfortably, try switching parts.

You can see the relationship between the two parts from Kuku on the next chart. We've put the second part below the first part, on the row where the feet usually go. But just because you don't see the feet on the chart, don't stop stepping the pulse on 1 and 3:

KUKU PARTS 1 & 2 (SOLO)   **TRACKS 9 & 1**

1	+	2	+	3	+	4	+	1	+	2	+	3	+	4	+
TT				TT				H		H		H	H		
TT		H	H				C	TT		H	H			C	

If you don't have a buddy handy, you can still practice putting the two parts together. Just slap one part while listening to the drum track of the other part. Remember, for easy reference all the drum tracks are listed on the face of the CD.

P = patty

To do the buddy version of the second part from Kuku, just replace each double thigh on 1 with a patty. **Patty** is short for "patty-cake." All you do is slap palms with your buddy with your arms out in front of you at chest height.

Here's the chart:

KUKU PART 2 (BUDDY)   **TRACKS 7 & 8**

1	+	2	+	3	+	4	+	1	+	2	+	3	+	4	+
P		H	H				C	P		H	H			C	
🦶				🦶				🦶				🦶			

If you've got three or more slappers, you can do this part in a circle. That's because patties – like flips – can be done to the side. So whenever the only contact in a buddy part is on patties you can do the part in a circle.

Now you know the buddy versions of both parts from Kuku. That means if you've got at least four people you can do both buddy parts at the same time. One pair slaps part 1 and the other slaps part 2.

Here's what the two buddy versions look like on a single chart. Again we've put the second part below the first and left out the feet:

SLAPPING PRINCIPLE

Whenever the only contact in a buddy part is on patties you can do the part in a circle.

KUKU PARTS 1 & 2 (BUDDY)   **TRACKS 9 & 1**

1	+	2	+	3	+	4	+	1	+	2	+	3	+	4	+
F				F				H		H		H	H		
P		H	H			C		P		H	H			<u>C</u>	

Once you've got the timing and basic moves down for Kuku, go ahead and loosen up. Personalize your part. Turn it into a dance. Get out there and strut your stuff.

Personalize your part. Turn it into a dance. Get out there and strut your stuff.

Bomba

Now it's time to shift from Africa to the Caribbean. Bomba (BOHM-bah) is a rhythm from Puerto Rico with deep African roots. Originally it was played on empty steel barrels, but now it's usually played on hand drums and other percussion instruments. On Track 10 you can hear how the two parts you'll be learning sound on conga drums – wooden barrel-shaped drums with calf-skin drumheads. To spice things up a little, we've added a clave to track 10 – that's the other intrument you'll hear.

The first part from Bomba is a two-measure pattern. To make it easier to learn, we've broken it in half. After you slap each half separately, you'll put the two together.

Here's the first half. Notice that the second step comes right in between the two pairs of hearts:

BOMBA PART 1 – FIRST HALF (SOLO) TRACK 11

1	+	2	+	3	+	4	+
C		H	H		H	H	
🦶				🦶			

Here's the second half. It's got a new move. Well, sort of. The "**T**" stands for a single **thigh**, which just means that you slap one thigh with one hand. You always do single thighs with alternating hands: first your right hand on your right thigh, then your left hand on your left thigh.

T = thigh

Notice that the first thigh falls on the AND of 2, right before your foot hits the floor on 3. We found it awkward to vocalize this pattern by calling out the moves because it's hard to repeat "thigh" four times in a row. So instead we used the phrase "**clap** . . . a-**bunch**-a-thighs":

BOMBA PART 1 – SECOND HALF (SOLO) TRACK 12

1	+	2	+	3	+	4	+
C			T	T	T	T	
🦶				🦶			

Now you're ready to put the two halves together and slap the complete first part from Bomba. Remember – if it's too hard to slap and step at the same time, just do the hand moves for now:

1	+	2	+	3	+	4	+	1	+	2	+	3	+	4	+
C		H	H		H	H		C				T	T	T	T
🦶				🦶				🦶				🦶			

S = slap

The buddy version of this part has a new move in it: the slap. A **slap** is like a high five, only lower – about shoulder height. With your elbow bent and your wrist and arm loose, just slap your buddy's hand in front of you. Slaps always come in pairs, and you always do them with alternating hands: first right, then left. As with all the moves, you should slap just hard enough to get a sound but not so hard that it hurts.

The slaps in the buddy version of the first part from Bomba come in the first measure, where they take the place of the first two hearts:

BOMBA PART 1 (BUDDY) TRACKS 13 & 14

1	+	2	+	3	+	4	+	1	+	2	+	3	+	4	+
C	S	S		H	H		C				T	T	T	T	
👣				👣				👣				👣			

If you goof up on a buddy pattern, no sweat. Just hop back in as soon as you can. Most of the time you can figure out what to do by copying your buddy. If you both mess up, go back and start over. Maybe you just need to slow down a little. If your timing is off, go back and take another look at the chart or listen to the slap track on the CD. Then try vocalizing the part for a while before you try slapping again. Whatever you do, don't criticize. Mobilize.

If your buddy goofs up, don't criticize. Mobilize.

Now for the second part from Bomba. Here's a warm-up exercise to get you started. It may help to notice that it has the same rhythm as the second measure of the part you just did – "**clap** . . . a-**bunch**-a-thighs." But here the moves are different – "**thighs** . . . clap-**clap**-heart-heart":

BOMBA PART 2 - WARM UP (SOLO) TRACK 15

1	+	2	+	3	+	4	+	1	+	2	+	3	+	4	+
TT				C	C	H	H	TT				C	C	H	H
👣				👣				👣				👣			

SLAPPING
PRINCIPLE

Vocalize while
you're slapping
until you know
the pattern.

To turn this pattern into the second part from Bomba, all you have to do is take out the second clap in each measure. To make sure you nail the clap on the AND of 2, it may help to include the step on 3 as part of your vocalization: "**thighs** . . . clap-**step**-heart-heart" or "**thighs** . . . clap-**foot**-heart-heart." It also helps to keep vocalizing while you're slapping:

BOMBA PART 2 (SOLO)   **TRACKS 16 & 17**

1	+	2	+	3	+	4	+	1	+	2	+	3	+	4	+
⫪			C	H	H			⫪			C	H	H		
👣				👣				👣				👣			

Now that you know how to slap both solo parts from Bomba, you can slap one part while your buddy slaps the other. Just remember to get in sync by counting and stepping together before you start slapping.

Here's what the two solo parts from Bomba look like together on a single chart:

BOMBA PARTS 1 & 2 (SOLO)   **TRACKS 18 & 10**

1	+	2	+	3	+	4	+	1	+	2	+	3	+	4	+
C		H	H		H	H		C				T	T	T	T
π		C		H	H			π		C		H	H		

If you've got three people, two of you can do the solo version of part 1 while the third person does the solo version of part 2. Or two of you can do the *buddy* version of part 1 while the third person does the solo version of part 2. Or one of you can slap part 1, another can slap part 2, and the third can slap a pizza in the oven. The point is: you've got lots of options.

To create the buddy version of part 2, all you do is replace the double thighs on 1 with patties:

BOMBA PART 2 (BUDDY)   **TRACKS 16 & 17**

1	+	2	+	3	+	4	+	1	+	2	+	3	+	4	+
P		C		H	H			P		C		H	H		
👣				👣				👣				👣			

Remember, since you only make contact with your buddy on patties on this part, you can do it in a circle.

Here's what the two buddy parts from Bomba look like on a single chart:

1	+	2	+	3	+	4	+	1	+	2	+	3	+	4	+
C		S	S		H	H		C				T	T	T	T
P			C		H	H		P			C		H	H	

If you've got some percussionists among you, have them play along while you slap. You don't even need real instruments; you can create your own. An empty soda pop can with a handful of rice in it makes a decent shaker. And overturned wastebaskets, paint buckets, or five-gallon plastic water bottles make great drums. Remember, Bomba was originally played in Puerto Rico on empty steel barrels, so there are no rules here and no limits on your imagination.

Conga

Now we're going to make a short hop from the island of Puerto Rico to the island of Cuba. The rhythm you're going to learn has the same name as the drum it's played on: Conga. This spicy rhythm is traditionally played at the Cuban Carnaval celebration.

In this lesson, instead of learning just two parts from Conga, you're going to learn three. You can hear all three parts played on conga drums on Track 19.

The first part you're going to learn is four measures long. That's twice as long as anything you've done so far! But you should have no trouble with it because it's a rhythm you've probably heard somewhere before – like on an old episode of *I Love Lucy*. And you can hear it slapped now on Track 20 and drummed on Track 22.

To notate it on a single chart we've simply added another hand row. When you get to the end of the first hand row just continue on to the second hand row without missing a beat. And when you get to the end of the second hand row, go back and start over. The stepping stays the same throughout – you step on each pulse:

CONGA PART 1 (SOLO) TRACKS 20 & 22

1	+	2	+	3	+	4	+	1	+	2	+	3	+	4	+
T				T				T		C					
T		T		T		T		T		C					
👣				👣				👣				👣			

The only tricky thing about slapping this part is getting the timing right on the claps. Each clap falls on the AND of 2, *just before* a pulse. But you can handle it. You've already clapped the AND of 2 in Bomba. And you should have no trouble handling the empty space *after* the claps as long as you keep a steady pulse going in your feet. So give it a try now.

✱ = splash

Once you're comfortable with the timing of this part, you're ready to try a new move: the splash. To make a **splash** you need to use your hands *and* your voice. Just throw your hands up in the air and at the same time make a splashing sound – sort of like the sound of a crash cymbal in a drumset: "Pshhhh." You'll hear how we do it on Track 21 when we replace the last clap in this part with a splash:

1	+	2	+	3	+	4	+	1	+	2	+	3	+	4	+
T				T				T				C			
T		T		T		T		T				✱			
👣				👣				👣				👣			

By the way, you don't have to use the sound we came up with for the splash. You can make any sound you want – as long as you make it at the right time. And when you're slapping with other people, you'll get the best effect if everyone makes the same sound, whatever that is.

Now here's the buddy version of this part. Since you only make contact on patties, it's another pattern you can do in a circle if you've got three or more people:

CONGA PART 1 (BUDDY)   TRACKS 21 & 22

1	+	2	+	3	+	4	+	1	+	2	+	3	+	4	+
⊤				C				P		C					
⊤		C		P		C		⊤		✳					
🦶				🦶				🦶				🦶			

We've also put a splash in the *second* part from Conga – on 4 in the second measure. The only tricky thing about this part is the timing of the hearts. When you look at the chart and when you listen to Track 23, notice that each pair of hearts starts on the beat *before* the pulse and ends *on* the pulse:

CONGA PART 2 (SOLO)   TRACKS 23 & 24

1	+	2	+	3	+	4	+	1	+	2	+	3	+	4	+
⊤		C		C				H	H			H	H		✳
🦶				🦶				🦶				🦶			

Now that you know both the first and second solo parts from Conga, you and a buddy can slap them at the same time. You might be wondering how to do that, since the first part is twice as long as the second. No problem. Just have whoever's doing the second part repeat it twice for every one repetition of the first. That's what you'll hear on Track 25. Everything else you know about combining parts stays the same.

To show the relationship between two parts we usually combine them on a single chart. But since these parts from Conga are of unequal length, we've put one chart on top of the other instead. To simplify the charts we've left off the foot rows, but of course you should keep stepping the pulse:

CONGA PART 1 WITH SPLASH (SOLO)   TRACKS 25 & 19

1	+	2	+	3	+	4	+	1	+	2	+	3	+	4	+
Π				Π				Π		C					
Π		Π		Π		Π		Π		*					

CONGA PART 2 (SOLO)   TRACKS 25 & 19

1	+	2	+	3	+	4	+	1	+	2	+	3	+	4	+
Π		C		C			H	H			H	H		*	

Here's the basic buddy version of the second part. All that's different from the solo version is that we've replaced the claps with flips:

CONGA BASIC PART 2 (BUDDY)   TRACKS 23 & 24

1	+	2	+	3	+	4	+	1	+	2	+	3	+	4	+
Π		F		F			H	H			H	H		*	
🦶				🦶				🦶				🦶			

To add more moves to the buddy version of this part, you can replace the second pair of hearts with slaps:

CONGA PART 2 (BUDDY)   TRACKS 23 & 24

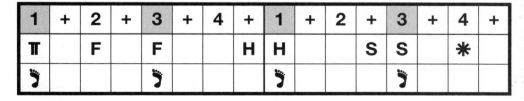

1	+	2	+	3	+	4	+	1	+	2	+	3	+	4	+
Π		F		F			H	H			S	S		*	
🦶				🦶				🦶				🦶			

Now that you know buddy versions for both the first and the second parts from Conga, if you've got four or more people you can slap the two buddy parts at the same time. Here are the two charts without the foot rows:

CONGA PART 1 (BUDDY) — TRACKS 25 & 19

1	+	2	+	3	+	4	+	1	+	2	+	3	+	4	+
Π				C				P		C					
Π		C		P		C		Π		✱					

CONGA PART 2 (BUDDY) — TRACKS 25 & 19

1	+	2	+	3	+	4	+	1	+	2	+	3	+	4	+
Π		F		F				H	H			S	S		✱

Before we get to the third part from Conga, we're going to take a moment to talk about the way we've been counting. All the rhythms you've been slapping so far have been counted in **cut-time**. In cut-time there are two pulses in each measure, and each pulse is divided into four eighth notes:

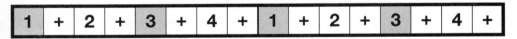

1 measure in cut-time   1 measure in cut-time

We also could have counted these rhythms in **4/4 time**. In 4/4, a measure is divided into four quarter note pulses, and each quarter note is divided into four sixteenth notes:

1 measure in 4/4

If we stack these charts one on top of the other, you can see that two measures of cut-time and one measure of 4/4 are the same length, and both have four pulses divided into four beats each. The only thing that's different is the counting system. Musicians commonly say that a rhythm counted either way is in **four**:

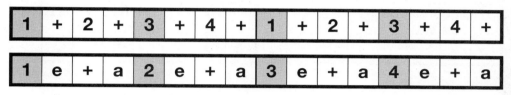

4/4

We like charting rhythms in four in cut-time rather than 4/4 for a lot of reasons. First, we find it easier to work with two short 8-beat measures rather than with one long 16-beat measure. We also like the counting system in cut-time better because it gives you a number as a reference point every two beats instead of every four. And we find it easier and more natural to talk about rhythms in cut-time. We'd feel silly talking about the "ee" of 3 or the "uh" of 4. And finally, Afro-Caribbean rhythms are traditionally counted in cut-time. So this is our roundabout way of explaining why you've been stepping the pulse on 1 and 3 instead of 1, 2, 3, and 4. Just thought you might be wondering.

All right, now for the third part from Conga. It's got a new move in it: the **snap**. All you do is snap your fingers. Snaps are done one hand at a time – first right then left – like hearts or single thighs. (If you're one of those people who just can't snap, do single thighs instead.)

X = snap

You'll snap twice in each measure of this part. The measures are identical except for the placement of the first snap. In the first measure it falls on 1, and in the second it falls on the AND of 1:

CONGA PART 3 (SOLO) TRACKS 26 & 27

1	+	2	+	3	+	4	+	1	+	2	+	3	+	4	+
X			X	H		H			X		X	H		H	
🦶				🦶					🦶			🦶			

Now that you know *three* solo parts from Conga, if you've got *three* or more people you can slap them all at the same time. You can hear how that sounds on Track 28. Here are all three charts stacked:

CONGA PART 1 WITH SPLASH (SOLO) TRACKS 28 & 19

1	+	2	+	3	+	4	+	1	+	2	+	3	+	4	+
𝕋				𝕋				𝕋		C					
𝕋	𝕋	𝕋	𝕋	𝕋		𝕋		𝕋		*					

CONGA PART 2 (SOLO) TRACKS 28 & 19

1	+	2	+	3	+	4	+	1	+	2	+	3	+	4	+
𝕋	C	C			H	H			H	H				*	

CONGA PART 3 (SOLO) TRACKS 28 & 19

1	+	2	+	3	+	4	+	1	+	2	+	3	+	4	+
X			X	H		H		X			X	H		H	

All you do to get the buddy version of the third part is replace the snaps with slaps:

CONGA PART 3 (BUDDY) TRACK 26 & 27

1	+	2	+	3	+	4	+	1	+	2	+	3	+	4	+
S			S	H		H			S		S	H		H	
🦶				🦶				🦶				🦶			

Finally, here are the charts for all three *buddy* parts:

CONGA PART 1 (BUDDY) TRACKS 28 & 19

1	+	2	+	3	+	4	+	1	+	2	+	3	+	4	+
𝕋				C				P		C					
𝕋		C		P		C		𝕋		✳					

CONGA PART 2 (BUDDY) TRACKS 28 & 19

1	+	2	+	3	+	4	+	1	+	2	+	3	+	4	+
𝕋		F		F			H	H			S	S		✳	

CONGA PART 3 (BUDDY) TRACKS 28 & 19

1	+	2	+	3	+	4	+	1	+	2	+	3	+	4	+
S			S	H		H			S		S	H		H	

Now that you've learned a total of seven different rhythmic patterns – two from Kuku, two from Bomba, and three from Conga – you should be able to slap your way through just about any song in four. So put on your favorite music and see if any you can slap along using any of the patterns you know. It probably makes sense to pick a song that's not too fast, but if you're into speed, go for it.

SLAPPING PRINCIPLE

Slap along with recorded music.

Lesson

Sunguru Bani

Sunguru Bani (soon-goo-roo bah-nee) is a dance rhythm from Mali, another country in West Africa. It's played at social gatherings and celebrations on djembes and various other drums and percussion instruments. You can hear how the three parts you'll be learning sound on djembes on Track 29.

If Track 29 sounds a little confusing at first, it's partly because Sunguru Bani isn't played in four, like all the other rhythms you've learned so far. It's played in **six**, an unfamiliar time signature for most Western ears.

Six is short for **6/8 time**. In 6/8 time, there are six eighth notes to a measure and the pulse falls on beats 1 and 4. Each of our charts in six is two measures long:

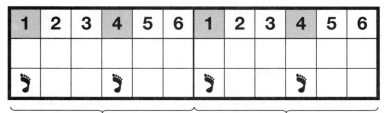

1	2	3	4	5	6	1	2	3	4	5	6
👣			👣			👣			👣		

$\underbrace{\hspace{4cm}}$ 1 measure in 6/8 $\qquad$ $\underbrace{\hspace{4cm}}$ 1 measure in 6/8

As you can see, on our charts in six there are four pulses, just like on our charts in four. What's different is that while each pulse in four is divided into *four* beats, each pulse in six is divided into *three*.

To help you get the feel of six, we're going to start with a couple of warm-up exercises. In both of them you'll be stepping the pulse and filling in all the beats in between with hand moves.

Here's the first one. It's a solo pattern. Start by counting out loud while you step the pulse on 1 and 4. As you count, accent the pulse in your voice: "**1**, 2, 3, **4**, 5, 6 ..." When you're ready, add the hands:

SIX WARM-UP (SOLO)　　　　　　　　　　　　**TRACK 30**

1	2	3	4	5	6	1	2	3	4	5	6
	T	T		H	H		T	T		H	H
👣			👣			👣			👣		

We've created a buddy version of this warm-up pattern by replacing the two thighs in the second measure with slaps:

SIX WARM-UP (BUDDY)　　　　　　　　　　　　**TRACK 30**

1	2	3	4	5	6	1	2	3	4	5	6
	T	T		H	H		S	S		H	H
👣			👣			👣			👣		

Now for the first part from Sunguru Bani. Notice that not every beat has a move on it – beat 6 in each measure is empty. Keep counting while you slap until you learn to feel the length of the silence of that empty beat:

SUNGURU BANI PART 1 (SOLO) **TRACKS 31 & 33**

1	2	3	4	5	6	1	2	3	4	5	6
	T	T		C			T	T		C	
👣			👣			👣			👣		

Learn to feel the length of the silence of the empty beat.

Now you're going to vary the first part by doing something different in the second measure. Instead of thighs you'll do hearts, and instead of a clap you'll do a splash. This is the version of part 1 we'll be using when we combine parts a little later:

SUNGURU BANI PART 1 (SOLO) **TRACKS 32 & 33**

1	2	3	4	5	6	1	2	3	4	5	6
	T	T		C			H	H		✳	
👣			👣			👣			👣		

To create the buddy version of this part, just replace the thighs and hearts with slaps:

SUNGURU BANI PART 1 (BUDDY) **TRACKS 32 & 33**

1	2	3	4	5	6	1	2	3	4	5	6
	S	S		C			S	S		✳	
👣			👣			👣			👣		

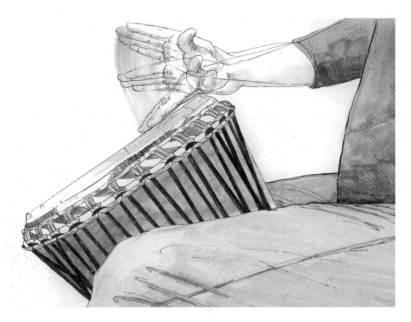

The second part from Sunguru Bani also has an empty beat: beat 2. Keep counting out loud while you do this part until your body knows exactly when to do the clap:

SUNGURU BANI PART 2 (SOLO)   **TRACKS 34 & 35**

1	2	3	4	5	6	1	2	3	4	5	6
		C		H	H			C		H	H
👣			👣			👣			👣		

Now that you know two solo parts from Sunguru Bani, you can slap one while your buddy slaps the other. Since both parts are the same length, we've gone back to putting them on a single chart:

1	2	3	4	5	6	1	2	3	4	5	6
	T	T		C			H	H		∗	
		C		H	H			C		H	H

To create the buddy version of the second part, just replace the hearts with slaps:

SUNGURU BANI PART 2 (BUDDY)   TRACKS 34 & 35

1	2	3	4	5	6	1	2	3	4	5	6
		C		S	S			C		S	S
👣			👣			👣			👣		

Here are the first two buddy parts on a single chart:

SUNGURU BANI PARTS 1 & 2 (BUDDY)   TRACKS 36 & 29

1	2	3	4	5	6	1	2	3	4	5	6
	S	S		C			S	S		∗	
		C		S	S			C		S	S

The third part from Sunguru Bani starts with a clap on beat 1 at the same time as you step. Then you do three thighs in a row: right-left-right. Notice that the middle thigh – the one you do with your left hand – coincides with the step on the pulse on 4:

1	2	3	4	5	6	1	2	3	4	5	6
C		T	T	T		C		T	T	T	
👣			👣			👣			👣		

Here are all three parts on a single chart. Notice how the clap moves from part to part on beats 1, 3, and 5 until it's replaced by a splash in the first part at the end of the second measure:

SUNGURU BANI PARTS 1, 2, & 3 (SOLO)   TRACKS 39 & 29

1	2	3	4	5	6	1	2	3	4	5	6
	T	T		C			H	H		✱	
		C		H	H			C		H	H
C		T	T	T		C		T	T	T	

If you replace the splash at the end of the first part with another clap, you get a consistent sequence of claps running throughout the rhythm on beats 1, 3, and 5 in both measures. These 6 evenly-spaced claps create the feeling of a competing pulse over the 4 evenly-spaced steps in your feet:

SUNGURU BANI PARTS 1, 2, & 3 (SOLO)   TRACKS 40 & 29

1	2	3	4	5	6	1	2	3	4	5	6
	T	T		C			H	H		C	
		C		H	H			C		H	H
C		T	T	T		C		T	T	T	

This relationship between the claps and the steps creates the **polyrhythm** of 6 over 4. If you think of it one measure at a time, then the polyrhythm is 3 over 2 – each measure has 3 evenly-spaced claps over 2 evenly-spaced steps. You can experience the polyrhythm of 3 over 2 in your own body by stepping the pulse on 1 and 4 and then adding claps on beats 1, 3, and 5. It may help to think of the pattern – or even vocalize it – as "**together**, clap-**step**-clap, ...":

THE POLYRHYTHM OF 3 OVER 2   TRACK 41

1	2	3	4	5	6	1	2	3	4	5	6
C		C		C		C		C		C	
𝟑			𝟑			𝟑			𝟑		

Now back to Sunguru Bani. The buddy version of the third part is a fun one. You're going to replace the three thighs with a new combination move: the slap-clap-slap. All you do is slap right, then clap, then slap left. Notice that in this part, the clap in the middle of the slap-clap-slap falls on the pulse on 4. Also notice that now you're clapping on every pulse. Since this gives the part a different sound, we recorded it on Track 42:

SUNGURU BANI PART 3 (BUDDY)   TRACKS 42 & 38

1	2	3	4	5	6	1	2	3	4	5	6
C		S	C	S		C		S	C	S	
𝟑			𝟑			𝟑			𝟑		

Here are all three buddy parts on a single chart:

1	2	3	4	5	6	1	2	3	4	5	6
	S	S		C			S	S		*	
		C		S	S			C		S	S
C		S	C	S		C		S	C	S	

Remember, even if you don't have enough people to do all three buddy parts together, you can always slap along with one of the drum parts on Track 33, 35, or 38.

Lesson **5**

Kpegisu

Kpegisu (peh-GEE-soo) is a rhythm in six from the West African country of Ghana. It's traditionally played at festivals and other gatherings along with singing and dancing. In this lesson, in addition to learning how to slap one of the drum parts from Kpegisu, you're also going to learn how to slap the cowbell part around which the rhythm is organized. You can hear how the drum part and the cowbell part sound together on Track 44. We also added a bass drum on the pulse to help you keep oriented in time.

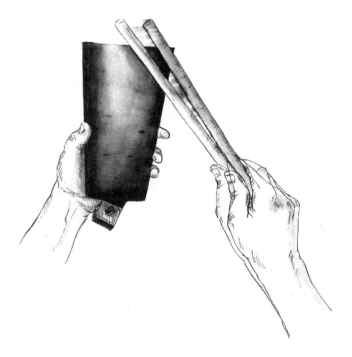

We're going to start with the cowbell part, which you can hear all by itself in an extended recording on Track 45. This beautiful rhythmic pattern is found in music all over the world. It's often called "the 6/8 bell," which is what we'll be calling it here. In Kpegisu – and in many other African and Afro-Cuban rhythms – the 6/8 bell serves as a **timeline** or reference rhythm for all the players in an ensemble.

A timeline is always played on an instrument that everyone can easily hear – like a cowbell – and it repeats without variation – like a metronome. But unlike the *uniform* clicks of a metronome – each indistinguishable from the next – a timeline is an *asymmetrical* pattern with its own distinct shape. It not only tells you how fast to go, it also tells you where you are in time. This is especially important in African and Afro-Cuban rhythms, where complex overlapping parts make it easy for you to lose your way. If you know how your part fits with the timeline, you can always find your place.

Because the 6/8 bell is a little more complex than the patterns you've learned so far, we're going to work our way up to it in four steps. The first three steps are exercises designed to get you ready for the fourth step, which is the 6/8 bell pattern itself. You'll do each step as a solo pattern. Once you've learned the complete 6/8 bell as a solo part, we'll show you the buddy version.

Step 1 starts on 6 in the second measure and both measures are the same. So start counting and stepping the pulse and then come in with the first thigh on 6 in the second measure. When you vocalize this pattern, you may find it helpful to include the step on 4 – "thigh-**thigh**, clap-**step** ...":

6/8 BELL – STEP 1 (SOLO)   TRACK 46

1	2	3	4	5	6	1	2	3	4	5	6
T		C			T	T		C			<u>T</u>
👣			👣			👣			👣		

Step 2 starts with the same three hand moves as step 1 and then moves on to two pairs of hearts:

6/8 BELL - STEP 2 (SOLO) TRACK 47

1	2	3	4	5	6	1	2	3	4	5	6
T		C		H	H		H	H			<u>T</u>
🦶			🦶			🦶			🦶		

Step 3 gives you the last piece in the puzzle of the 6/8 bell. The first clap in each measure comes right *after* the pulse while the second clap falls right *on* the pulse:

6/8 BELL - STEP 3 (SOLO) TRACK 48

1	2	3	4	5	6	1	2	3	4	5	6
	C		C				C		C		
🦶			🦶			🦶			🦶		

Now just slide a piece of step 3 into the second measure of step 2, and the puzzle of the 6/8 bell is complete. Notice that on the pulse on 1 in the first measure and 4 in the second you step and make a hand move at the same time. Also notice that you start clapping on 6 in the second measure. Although the actual bell pattern you'll hear on Track 45 starts on 1, we have you start one beat earlier so you can keep the two single thighs together:

6/8 BELL (SOLO) TRACKS 49 & 45

1	2	3	4	5	6	1	2	3	4	5	6
T		C		H	H		C		C		<u>T</u>
🦶			🦶			🦶			🦶		

To create the buddy version of the 6/8 bell, just replace the two hearts with slaps:

6/8 BELL (BUDDY)   **TRACKS 49 & 45**

1	2	3	4	5	6	1	2	3	4	5	6
T		C		S	S		C		C		T
👣			👣			👣			👣		

The drum part you're going to learn from Kpegisu is played with sticks on a small wooden drum called a kagan (kah-gahn). We recorded this part on a larger Ghanaian drum along with the bell part on Track 44. The solo slapping version is pure thighs. After the second pulse, all you do is fill in the beats between steps:

KPEGISU DRUM PART (SOLO)   **TRACKS 50 & 44**

1	2	3	4	5	6	1	2	3	4	5	6
				T	T		T	T		T	T
👣			👣			👣			👣		

Now grab a buddy and one of you slap the 6/8 bell while the other slaps the drum part. Since a timeline establishes the framework of a rhythm, whoever's slapping the 6/8 bell should start first. After a couple repetitions, the person who's slapping the drum part should come in on 5 in the first measure. That's what you'll hear us do on Track 51.

Here are the two parts on a single chart. Notice that the two parts come together on 5 and 6 in the first measure:

6/8 BELL & KPEGISU DRUM PART (SOLO)   **TRACKS 51 & 44**

1	2	3	4	5	6	1	2	3	4	5	6
T		C		H	H		C		C		<u>T</u>
				T	T		T	T		T	T

Here's the buddy version of the drum part:

KPEGISU DRUM PART (BUDDY)   **TRACKS 50 & 44**

1	2	3	4	5	6	1	2	3	4	5	6
			S	S			H	H		T	T
👣			👣			👣			👣		

If you've got four or more slappers, you can now combine the buddy versions of the 6/8 bell and the drum part. Here are both parts on a single chart. Since they both have slaps on 5 and 6 in the first measure, that's a perfect place to check in to make sure you're slapping in sync:

6/8 BELL & KPEGISU DRUM PART (BUDDY)   **TRACKS 49 & 45**

1	2	3	4	5	6	1	2	3	4	5	6
T		C		S	S		C		C		<u>T</u>
				S	S		H	H		T	T

Drummers in a traditional African ensemble usually have some freedom to vary their parts within limits. Sometimes this means adding notes, but just as often it means leaving notes out to create space in a part.

One way to vary the drum part from Kpegisu is to leave out the middle pair of thighs. That means you'll be doing thighs only on 5 and 6 in both measures:

KPEGISU DRUM PART VARIATION (SOLO) TRACK 52

1	2	3	4	5	6	1	2	3	4	5	6
				T	T					T	T
👣			🎵			👣			🎵		

Now that you know two variations of the drum part, you can alternate between them to create a four-measure phrase. You'll find that longer phrase on the next chart. Below it is a chart of the 6/8 bell so your buddy can slap along with you. On Track 53 you can hear how the two parts sound slapped together. If you don't have a buddy handy, you can slap the drum part variations along with the actual 6/8 bell on Track 45:

KPEGISU DRUM PART VARIATIONS (SOLO) TRACK 53

1	2	3	4	5	6	1	2	3	4	5	6
				T	T					T	T
				T	T	T	T			T	T

6/8 BELL (SOLO) TRACK 53

1	2	3	4	5	6	1	2	3	4	5	6
T		C		H	H		C		C		T̲

By the way, these drum part variations are ideal for slapping while you walk. Since they only involves thighs, you won't have to worry about anyone looking at you funny or thinking you're weird. With your hands down low, who's going to know?

Here's the buddy version of the drum part variations. We've put a chart of the buddy version of the 6/8 bell below it:

KPEGISU DRUM PART VARIATIONS (BUDDY)   TRACK 53

1	2	3	4	5	6	1	2	3	4	5	6
				S	S					T	T
				S	S		H	H		T	T

6/8 BELL (BUDDY)   TRACK 53

1	2	3	4	5	6	1	2	3	4	5	6
T		C		S	S		C		C		T

Before we leave this lesson, we can't resist pointing out something really cool about the relationship between the 6/8 bell and the major scale. If you don't know what the major scale is, this isn't going to mean a thing to you, so you're excused. But for those of you who are still with us, check this out.

Think of a row of boxes on one of our charts in six as the keys on a piano, with the first box in the row as middle C. If you put the 6/8 bell pattern on that row, the notes of the bell pattern fall on what would be all the white keys on the piano. Where there are empty boxes on the chart, there would be black keys on the piano:

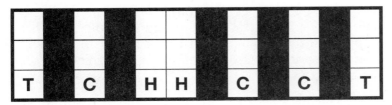

Is this just a coincidence? Or does it reflect some mysterious underlying unity between rhythm and melody? We haven't got a clue. But it's an interesting question, isn't it?

Lesson **6**

The One-Bar Clave

In this last lesson, you're going to do something new with your feet. Instead of stepping the pulse, you'll be stepping a dynamic rhythm that's found in music all over the world. In Afro-Cuban music it's called the one-bar clave (CLAH-vay).

Clave means "timeline" as well as the instrument it's played on. Claves are two cylindrical pieces of wood that are struck together to produce a crisp, penetrating click:

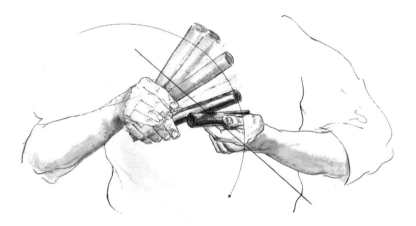

You can can hear the one-bar clave played on claves on Track 54. After four measures, we've added a bass drum to give the track some bottom.

Before you try stepping the one-bar clave, take a look at its structure on the next chart. We've left off the hand row so you can focus on the feet. Notice the pattern repeats twice on a two-measure chart ("bar" in "one-bar" means "measure"):

1	+	2	+	3	+	4	+	1	+	2	+	3	+	4	+
👣			👣			👣		👣			👣			👣	

Evenly-spaced　　　　　Hitch

The pattern is like a wheel that's not quite round; it's got a hitch in it. It starts with three evenly spaced notes. Then comes the hitch, and the pattern abruptly starts over again on 1. This uneven-ness makes the one-bar clave more difficult to step than the pulse, but it gives the pattern tremendous vitality and forward momentum.

The easiest way to learn the one-bar clave footdance is to start by counting out loud and accenting the pattern in your voice: "1 AND 2 **AND** 3 AND 4 AND 1 ..." Then keep counting while you start stepping the pattern. You can start with either foot, just as you can when you step the pulse. But since there's an odd number of steps in each measure, if you start with your right foot in the first measure, you'll start with your left in the second:

ONE-BAR CLAVE FOOTDANCE (SOLO)　　　　　TRACK 55

1	+	2	+	3	+	4	+	1	+	2	+	3	+	4	+
👣			👣			👣		👣			👣			👣	

WARNING:
One-bar clave stepping has been shown to induce the spontaneous formation of conga lines. To prevent injury, push all furniture back before attempting this pattern in a group.

Now it's time to add your hands. You're going to fill in the space between the first two steps with hearts and put a clap on 3. Start by counting and stepping before you add your hands:

ADDING THE HANDS (SOLO)   **TRACK 56**

1	+	2	+	3	+	4	+	1	+	2	+	3	+	4	+
	H	H		C					H	H		C			
🦶			🦶			🦶		🦶			🦶			🦶	

Guess what? You've been clapping the **backbeat**, which is every second pulse. From rock to pop to funk to hip-hop, the backbeat is the backbone of almost all dance music.

From rock to pop to funk to hip-hop, the backbeat is the backbone of almost all dance music.

On a drumset, the backbeat is usually played on a snare drum using a technique called a rimshot, which produces a loud crack. We've used a clap to accent the backbeat in this pattern because it's the closest you can get to a rimshot with your bare hands.

Now add a splash on 4 in the second measure to vary the pattern:

ADDING A SPLASH (SOLO)   **TRACK 57**

1	+	2	+	3	+	4	+	1	+	2	+	3	+	4	+
	H	H		C					H	H		C		✳	
🦶			🦶			🦶		🦶			🦶			🦶	

To create the buddy version of this pattern, just replace the second pair of hearts with slaps:

ADDING A SPLASH (BUDDY)   TRACK 57

1	+	2	+	3	+	4	+	1	+	2	+	3	+	4	+
	H	H		C					S	S		C		✳	
👣			👣			👣		👣			👣			👣	

In the next pattern, you're going to go back to slapping solo and fill in *all* the beats between your steps. And instead of accenting the backbeat with a clap, you're going to accent the AND of 4:

FILLING IN ALL THE BEATS (SOLO)   TRACK 58

1	+	2	+	3	+	4	+	1	+	2	+	3	+	4	+
	T	T		H	H		C		T	T		H	H		C
👣			👣			👣		👣			👣			👣	

Now create a two-measure phrase by combining the first measure of the pattern you just did with the second measure of the previous solo pattern:

COMBINATION PATTERN 1 (SOLO)   TRACK 59

1	+	2	+	3	+	4	+	1	+	2	+	3	+	4	+
	T	T		H	H		C		H	H		C		✳	
👣			👣			👣		👣			👣			👣	

To create the buddy version of this pattern, just replace the hearts in the second measure with slaps:

COMBINATION PATTERN 1 (BUDDY) TRACK 59

1	+	2	+	3	+	4	+	1	+	2	+	3	+	4	+
	T	T		H	H		C		S	S		C		✳	
🦶			🦶			🦶		🦶				🦶		🦶	

SLAPPING
PRINCIPLE

Try switching
buddies in the
middle of a
pattern.

If you're slapping this pattern in a group, here's something fun to try. We call it switching buddies midstream. Right after you finish the slaps in the second measure, keep doing the pattern while you start moving towards a new partner. You've got until the slaps come around again to make contact with somebody new. This exercise tends to disintegrate into chaos pretty quickly, but what the heck.

Here's another buddy variation you can do with the one-bar clave footdance. It includes a new sequence of hand moves: the clap-patty-clap. Notice that on 4 in each measure you clap and step at the same time:

CLAP-PATTY-CLAP (BUDDY) TRACK 60

1	+	2	+	3	+	4	+	1	+	2	+	3	+	4	+
	T	T		C	P	C			T	T		C	P	C	
🦶			🦶			🦶		🦶				🦶		🦶	

In the first measure of the next pattern, you're going to add a patty to the clap-patty-clap to make it a clap-patty-clap-patty:

CLAP-PATTY-CLAP-PATTY (BUDDY)　　　　　　　　**TRACK 61**

1	+	2	+	3	+	4	+	1	+	2	+	3	+	4	+
	T	T		C	P	C	P		T	T		C	P	C	
👣			👣			👣		👣			👣			👣	

Here's another buddy pattern with another new sequence of hand moves: the clap-slap-clap-slap. You clap, slap right, clap, slap left. This sequence is easier done than said. If you don't believe us, try saying it really fast three times in a row. Then do the same with "bugs black blood." Then notice that both measures in the pattern are the same:

CLAP-SLAP-CLAP-SLAP (BUDDY)　　　　　　　　**TRACK 62**

1	+	2	+	3	+	4	+	1	+	2	+	3	+	4	+
	T	T		C	S	C	S		T	T		C	S	C	S
👣			👣			👣		👣			👣			👣	

You can create a two-measure pattern by combining the first measure from the pattern you just did with the second measure from the pattern before it. This two-measure pattern has the same rhythm as the clap-patty-clap-patty pattern that's recorded on Track 61:

COMBINATION PATTERN 2 (BUDDY)　　　　　　　　**TRACK 61**

1	+	2	+	3	+	4	+	1	+	2	+	3	+	4	+
	T	T		C	S	C	S		T	T		C	P	C	
👣			👣			👣		👣			👣			👣	

The last buddy pattern creates a four-measure phrase by combining the pattern you just did with an earlier pattern. To make the chart compact, we've only included one foot row. So start by slapping the top hand row, next slap the hand row beneath it, and then start over.

If you've got at least two pairs of buddies, you can do this pattern as a round. First get in sync by having everybody do the one-bar clave footdance together. Then have the first pair of buddies start slapping the pattern. When they get to the second hand row, have the second pair start slapping at the beginning:

COMBINATION PATTERN 3 (BUDDY)   **TRACK 63**

1	+	2	+	3	+	4	+	1	+	2	+	3	+	4	+
	T	T		C	S	C	S		T	T		C	P	C	
	T	T		H	H		C		S	S		C		✳	
🦶			🦶		🦶		🦶			🦶		🦶			

We've taken you as far as we can for now. But we've only slapped the surface. Dig into the sources in the next section for more rhythms and inspiration. In the meantime – if you haven't already – start making up your own moves and patterns. If you want to, you can write them down on the blank charts on pages 65–67. Then add songs, sounds, raps, or rhymes. Go nuts. Slap yourself silly.

Slap yourself silly.

Sources for further study

Instructional books and videos on djembe and West African rhythms

African Percussion – The Djembe by Serge Blanc (book with CD).

A Life for the Djembe by Mamady Keita (book with CD)

How to Play Djembe – West African Rhythms for Beginners by Alan Dworsky and Betsy Sansby (book with CD)

The Rhythms of Guinea, West Africa (Volumes 1 & 2) with Karamba Diabate (videos).

Show Me the Rhythms for Jembe (Volumes 1 & 2) with Kalani (videos).

Traditional Rhythms of the Malinke (Volumes 1 & 2) with Mamady Keita (videos)

CDs of djembe and West African drumming

Adam Drame: Mandingo Drums Volumes 1 and 2

Famadou Konate: Malinke Rhythms and Songs

Farafina: Faso Denou and Bolomakote

Fatala: Gongoma Times

Mamady Keita: Wassolon, Nankama, Mogobalu, Afo, Balandugu Kan, and Mamady Lee

Ensemble National de la Republique de Guinee: Les Ballets Africains

Les Percussions de Guinee: Volumes 1 and 2

Instructional books and videos on conga and Afro-Cuban rhythms

Advanced Conga with Rolando Soto (video)

All About Bongos with Kalani (video)

Conga Drumming – A Beginner's Guide to Playing with Time by Alan Dworsky and Betsy Sansby (book with CD)

Mozambique (Volumes 1 & 2) with Kim Atkinson (videos)

Rumba Guaguanco Conversations by Arturo Rodriquez (book with CD)

Show Me the Rhythms for Bongos with Kalani (video)

The Essence of Afro-Cuban Percussion and Drumset by Ed Uribe (book with 2 CDs)

CDs of conga and Afro-Cuban drumming

Afro Cuba: A Musical Anthology (Rounder Records)

Los Munequitos de Matanzas: Congo Yambumba, Oyelos de Nuevo, Rumba Caliente

Los Papines: Encuento de Tambores, Homenaje a Mis Colegas, Oye Men Listen – Guaguanco, Rumba Sin Alare, Tambores Cubanos

Sabu: Palo Conga

Totico y sus Rumberos: Totico y sus Rumberos

Blank charts

1	+	2	+	3	+	4	+	1	+	2	+	3	+	4	+
👣				👣				👣				👣			

1	+	2	+	3	+	4	+	1	+	2	+	3	+	4	+
👣				👣				👣				👣			

1	+	2	+	3	+	4	+	1	+	2	+	3	+	4	+
👣				👣				👣				👣			

1	+	2	+	3	+	4	+	1	+	2	+	3	+	4	+
👣				👣				👣				👣			

1	+	2	+	3	+	4	+	1	+	2	+	3	+	4	+
👣				👣				👣				👣			

Blank charts

1	+	2	+	3	+	4	+	1	+	2	+	3	+	4	+

1	+	2	+	3	+	4	+	1	+	2	+	3	+	4	+

1	+	2	+	3	+	4	+	1	+	2	+	3	+	4	+

1	+	2	+	3	+	4	+	1	+	2	+	3	+	4	+

1	+	2	+	3	+	4	+	1	+	2	+	3	+	4	+

Blank charts

Chart 1

1	2	3	4	5	6	1	2	3	4	5	6
👣			👣			👣			👣		

Chart 2

1	2	3	4	5	6	1	2	3	4	5	6
👣			👣			👣			👣		

Chart 3

1	2	3	4	5	6	1	2	3	4	5	6
👣			👣			👣			👣		

Chart 4

1	2	3	4	5	6	1	2	3	4	5	6

Chart 5

1	2	3	4	5	6	1	2	3	4	5	6

Also available from Dancing Hands Music

$24.95

Conga Drumming
A Beginner's Guide to Playing with Time
BY ALAN DWORSKY AND BETSY SANSBY

This award-winning book and CD is a complete, step-by-step course on how to play congas. Right from the start you'll learn interlocking parts for several Afro-Caribbean rhythms, including Rumba, Bomba, Calypso, Conga, and Bembe. While you're learning the patterns, you'll also learn how to make all the basic strokes. We use life-like illustrations to show how each stroke looks from the outside and give detailed descriptions to explain how each stroke feels from the inside. We also use the simple charting system as in SLAP HAPPY. And you can hear how each drum part sounds on the CD that comes with the book.

"Fantastic!" – RHYTHM MAGAZINE

"There is no other source for this kind of information that is as simply and sensibly explained, and contains such a wealth of rhythms. CONGA DRUMMING welcomes rather than intimidates beginners. Dig into this book and in a very short time you will be playing well. Bravo and muchas gracias Alan and Betsy!"
– DRUM MAGAZINE

"The best book of its kind."
– ARTHUR HULL

World-Beat & Funk Grooves
Playing a Drumset the Easy Way
BY ALAN DWORSKY AND BETSY SANSBY

This book takes African, Afro-Cuban, and funk grooves and applies them to the drumset in a linear style. It uses an ingenious method that makes complex rhythms magically emerge out of simple sequences of body movements. Within days you'll be playing patterns that usually take months to master. It comes with 2 CDs: one contains samples of every pattern in the book, the other is a Timelines CD you can play along with while you practice.

"It doesn't get any more accessible than this"
– DRUM MAGAZINE

$24.95

Free sample lesson at
dancinghands.com

68

Conga Drumming
A Beginner's Video Guide

This video brings the book CONGA DRUMMING to life, and gives you a chance to see how all the basic patterns are supposed to be played. It's a great way to learn proper playing technique, because we teach each stroke using multiple camera angles and slow-motion photography. The video features instruction by Jorge Bermudez and performances by special guests Raul Rekow of Santana and Cuban dancer Rosie Lopez Moré.

"**A <u>must-see</u> for all beginners**."
– MICKEY HART

"**Slammin!** The best video for learning to play congas."
– CHALO EDUARDO, PERCUSSIONIST WITH
SERGIO MENDES

$29.95

Raul Rekow of **Santana** gives playing tips and solos on congas and bongos in the "burning performances by the ensemble."
– DRUM MAGAZINE

Hip Grooves for Hand Drums
How to play funk, rock & world-beat patterns on any drum

BY ALAN DWORSKY AND BETSY SANSBY

This is the book for hand drummers who want to play contemporary music. It's filled with great dance grooves, many of them adapted from drumset patterns used in rock, pop, and funk music. You can play these grooves on any hand drum – a djembe, a conga, or any drum where you can get both hands on the head. The CD that comes with the book has samples of all the patterns and extended tracks so you can play along. Whether you want to play in a band, jam in the park, or just drum along with your favorite CDs, this book will show you how, step by step.

$24.95

A Rhythmic Vocabulary
A Musician's Guide to Understanding and Improvising with Rhythm
BY ALAN DWORSKY AND BETSY SANSBY

This award-winning book is for any musician who wants to groove and solo with greater rhythmic freedom and understanding. It's the first systematic, comprehensive approach to the study of rhythm. It organizes and explains hundreds of African and Afro-Cuban patterns in step-by-step lessons to give you a deeper understanding of rhythmic structure. We also teach concepts and variation techniques you can use to create patterns of your own. The book comes with a Timelines CD for you to play along with while you practice. And CDs with samples of all the patterns in the book are now available at dancinghands.com.

"**A goldmine** ... Each new idea is introduced in a way that makes it seem like the easiest and most natural thing a player could do. A RHYTHMIC VOCABULARY promises to be a roadmap to rhythm for any musician and it delivers." – DRUM MAGAZINE

$29.95

Free sample lesson at dancinghands.com

Secrets of the Hand
Soloing Strategies for Hand Drummers
BY ALAN DWORSKY AND BETSY SANSBY

This book is for advanced hand drummers who want to play complex solos using simple sequences of hand strokes. Whether you play conga or djembe, the practical hand-pattern strategies explained here will help you get the most out of your hands with the least amount of effort. And whether you want to solo in a traditional African or Afro-Cuban ensemble, in a drum circle, in a band, or in your living room along with your favorite CDs, SECRETS OF THE HAND will help you take your playing to the next level.

$24.95

CD with samples of every pattern in **Secrets** now available at dancinghands.com

How to Play Djembe
West African Rhythms for Beginners
BY ALAN DWORSKY AND BETSY SANSBY

"**A superb work** ... it makes learning easy and fun, and Joh Camara's playing on the play-along CD is a joy to hear."
— PROFESSOR MICHAEL WILLIAMS, DEPARTMENT OF MUSIC, WINTHROP UNIVERSITY

This book and CD is a complete, step-by-step course on how to play djembe. Right from the start you'll learn inter-locking parts for some of the most popular West African rhythms: Kuku, Djole, Kassa, Madan, Suku, Sunguru Bani, and Tiriba. While you're learning the patterns, you'll also learn how to make all the basic strokes. We use life-like illustrations to show how each stroke looks from the outside and give detailed descriptions to explain how each stroke feels from the inside. We also use the simple charting system as in SLAP HAPPY.

$24.95

The CD that comes with the book gives you a chance to hear how each part sounds separately and how the parts for each rhythm fit together. It was recorded by Joh Camara, a master drummer from Bamako, Mali. Each rhythm lasts at least five minutes, so you'll have plenty of time to play along. And when Joh solos at the end of each track, you'll feel the thrill of playing your part along an ensemble and lead drummer.

Jaguar at Half Moon Lake
BY DANCING HANDS

"**A luminous debut**" – NEW MUSIC SERIES REVIEW

"**Gorgeous melodies and mesmerizing rhythms**"
– DIRTY LINEN

This CD of original music features Indie-award winning Dean Magraw on acoustic guitar and several world percussionists, including Congolese master drummer Coster Massamba on djembe. You can hear excerpts from Jaguar on track 64 of your SLAP HAPPY CD.

$13.95

We also carry lots of other instructional books and videos on hand drumming. You can call toll-free to order at
1-800-898-8036
or check out our full catalog and order online at
dancinghands.com

About the Authors

Alan Dworsky and *Betsy Sansby* were born in the 1950s ten blocks away from each other in St. Paul, Minnesota. Thirty years later they got married and they've been happily drumming together ever since. They are the authors of CONGA DRUMMING, HOW TO PLAY DJEMBE, HIP GROOVES FOR HAND DRUMS, WORLD-BEAT & FUNK GROOVES, A RHYTHMIC VOCABULARY, and SECRETS OF THE HAND.

We want to hear from you!

Now that SLAP HAPPY is in your hands, you're probably doing all sorts of moves and grooves we never dreamed of. So write to us and let us know what you're up to. If you want to show us, send us a home video. We might even be able to include a short clip in our upcoming SLAP HAPPY video.

Email:
al@dancinghands.com

Address:
DANCING HANDS MUSIC
4275 Churchill Circle
Minnetonka, MN 55345